WINDOW INTO A NEST

by Geraldine Lux Flanagan
and Sean Morris
Oxford Scientific Films

Kestrel Books

KESTREL BOOKS

Published by Penguin Books Ltd

Harmondsworth, Middlesex, England

Text and photographs copyright © 1975

by Geraldine Lux Flanagan and Oxford Scientific Films Ltd

First published 1975

ISBN 0 7226 5212 7

Printed in Great Britain by Westerham Press Ltd, Westerham, Kent

Foreword

This fascinating book literally throws a spotlight on a seemingly commonplace natural process that happens every spring all round us, yet passes unnoticed by most: the raising, by innumerable pairs of birds, of their offspring – for all organisms the most important achievement of their lives. Many of our birds build their nests in hidden places and so protect their vulnerable broods from adverse weather and above all from predation. But it is just this useful habit that makes it so difficult for us to observe their family life. Yet, as the authors show, one simple trick can secure us a ringside seat, from where we can follow all that normally happens in the utmost secrecy and in extremely dim light.

Window into a Nest is the outcome of close collaboration between two of my fellow naturalists whose work I have long admired. A chance event started them off. When, some years ago, I said somewhat casually to Sean Morris that 'a glass-backed nestbox might provide an attractive subject for a little film', he lost no time in putting up such a box on the window of his room in the headquarters of Oxford Scientific Films Ltd. Neither did the blue tits living round the building lose time in occupying the home so suddenly provided in an area where natural holes are at a premium. Concealed in a blacked-out hide indoors, Sean saw them inspect his box within a foot's distance from his face. Knowing that animals are rarely disturbed by brief light flashes for still photography, he began to take a few 'family snaps'.

When Geraldine Lux Flanagan, already widely known by her books *The First Nine Months of Life* and *Window into an Egg*, happened to see Sean's set-up and was allowed a peep inside, she suggested that his rehearsals for the planned filming could be used for the purpose of a book, and this was how their joint project began. Together they sat almost daily in front of their little 10p 'theatre', intently watching for many hours at a stretch and recording, in notebook after notebook and on over two thousand photographs, the entire sequence of events in the family life of one of our most colourful native birds. The film made later, and transmitted by Anglia TV in its *Survival* series, has in the meantime been enjoyed by numerous viewers. Both book and film were made without in the least disturbing either the parent birds or their young.

The story presented here, in which text and illustrations are equally essential, has some general implications. One is that our native fauna offers opportunities for 'home-based safaris' no less spectacular than those to nature reserves abroad. Although the nestbox trick is not as simple as it might sound, one can create numerous other opportunities of a similar kind, for instance by providing a feeding tray a few yards from one's window, or a shallow pond in the lawn; or one can offer temporary hospitality in a simple aquarium to equally beautiful creatures of our own inland waters, such as newts or sticklebacks. Another moral to be drawn from the book is that seeing really 'live', how animals go about their business, getting *any* first-hand glimpse of animal behaviour, may open a window to much more than just the one event that one happens to come across. It may awaken an interest in all natural phenomena, an extended awareness of one's surroundings that can last a lifetime, and that can help in fostering even in the most urbanized human being a sense of kinship with his fellow creatures. It is this sense of being part, rather than the undisputed, arrogant and ruthless master of all that lives, which, in the times to come, we may well need more than ever before.

NIKO TINBERGEN, F.R.S.
PROFESSOR EMERITUS OF ANIMAL BEHAVIOUR, UNIVERSITY OF OXFORD
NOBEL PRIZEWINNER 1973

Acknowledgements

We owe a profound debt to Professor Niko Tinbergen whose stimulating influence and teaching opened our eyes to the wide importance of the study of animal behaviour and led us to develop a special interest in the subject. We are therefore especially pleased that he leads the reader into this book through his Foreword with its thought-provoking conclusion. Professor Tinbergen very kindly read the manuscript for the book, and he contributed many vital suggestions and ideas to it.

We are most grateful also to Dr Christopher Perrins, Director of the Edward Grey Institute of Field Ornithology, University of Oxford. He gave us access to the University's comprehensive collection of scientific literature on the subject which was an invaluable aid in gathering information. Dr Perrins also read the manuscript and most helpfully advised us on scientific details. We wish in addition to thank Professor D.H. Morse and Dr J.N.M. Smith for their help in providing information.

During the months of photography we greatly appreciated the assistance of our colleagues at Oxford Scientific Films, David Thompson and Ian Moar. Mr S.A. Buckingham carried out the marathon task of developing and printing our total of well over 2000 photographs. Mr Michael Dudley expertly prepared the final prints for publication, with assistance from Mrs Pat Clarke.

But, of course, there would not have been any book without the participation of our blue tit family. If they could read, they would rightly feel that this is their book, not ours. We shall try to express our appreciation by putting out extra treats of suet for them in winter.

Contents

Nestbox – actual size

WINDOW INTO A NEST

The bird family lived undisturbed in their nest, with only window glass separating them from us. Here the mother was just arriving with food for her nearly full-grown chicks.

Secret World

Imagine you are stepping behind the special black curtains covering a window in a house in Oxfordshire to look – as we did last spring – into the secret world of one family of shy woodland birds living undisturbed in their nest.

Two blue tits, a hen and cock, came in February. Three months later, in June, a thriving family of nine flew out. During all that time we watched and photographed them every day and many nights. We saw, as you will see, how beautifully they co-operated and communicated with one another as they chose a place to nest, then furnished it, waited for the right season, then mated and produced a family, and gave their young constant care and protection.

To see the birds in their natural way of life, neither tame nor captive, we had to provide an outdoor place for them as similar as possible to a hidden nesting hole in a tree. For this we built a special wooden nesting box with a small entrance hole, no wider than a ten-pence piece, open to the surrounding countryside. The 'secret' of the box was that it had no back wall. Instead we fixed it to our window so that glass replaced the missing rear wall, and through this we had a clear view into the nest.

Peering into the indoor tent 'theatre': the nestbox on the darkened window seemed like a stage.

However, no bird tenants would have made themselves at home here if they could have seen us while we watched them. They needed to feel completely safe and private. Therefore we boarded up the window all round except for the one small area of clear glass at the centre which formed the 'see-through' back of the nest. In addition we built a shallow indoor tent of black cloth curtains to entirely cover the inside of our window and shield it from any light in the room. Inside the tent we were not in total black-out because a glimmer of light came in through the nest hole. Thus we were not entirely invisible, and had to be extra careful to avoid any give-away movements or noises on our side. We had to tiptoe in and out slowly and silently.

Sitting in the quiet darkness of the tent was very much like being in a small theatre with the birds on a stage before us. Gradually we learned to understand better how they organized their lives: how they responded to each other, to the world around them, to the seasons, to their food supplies, and also to dangers and possible enemies – as all creatures must do in order to survive, and for life to be carried forward from parents to young.

10

In learning so much about this one family of birds we not only got to know them as individuals with their own ways, we also learned a great deal which would be true of all higher animals – indeed including people. The key to the wider understanding were questions we always had in mind as we watched: 'why did he do this . . . why did she respond in that way . . . what was the result of their actions, what made them do it just on a certain day, in a certain way?'

As you turn the page you will meet our birds as we first caught sight of them near our house flitting from tree to tree, seemingly without purpose – until we looked more closely.

The outside of the window was boarded up all round the nestbox. The parents could fly freely to and from the surrounding woodland.

Winter Couple

Looking out from our window into the bare trees of late winter we learned to recognize two regular visitors among the branches. They were the two small birds who came to build their nest and raise a family in our window nestbox.

On warmer days, and especially in the mornings, we usually did not have to wait long before one of them came into sight flitting from branch to branch, now and then giving a brisk, cheerful four-note call *tsee, tsee, tsee, tsit!* Then we knew we could shortly expect to see the second bird following in friendly pursuit and announcing its presence with a similar call. After a few days we could tell these two apart from any other blue tits who occasionally flew by. By the colour of the edges of their wing feathers we knew that both birds were less than one year old, and that this would be their first experience of spring. But we could not tell by their feathers or shape whether one was male and the other female. Among these birds, and all their relatives, hen and cock look alike and are the same size. Nevertheless, simply by watching them closely to observe their actions – that is, their behaviour – it soon became easy to tell their sex, and know who was who.

On this particular morning in March the first bird had landed low on a tree opposite us. The choice of the lower branches made it likely that this was the hen. The second bird appeared shortly, landed higher up in the tree and then, in cock-like fashion, he swooped down aiming straight at the first bird. She was not put off by this apparent attack, as a fellow cock certainly would have been. Unperturbed, she nimbly hopped further down on the same branch to let the cock land where she had been. No doubt about it now, this was a hen, and surely a hen ready to receive her cock's attentions.

She hopped further down to let him land . . .

she vibrated her wings; he hopped close to her . . . ➤

She spread her wings and began to vibrate them slightly, and with this she uttered a soft twittering sound as only hens will do and only when they are encouraging one particular cock. Indeed the cock's attention was captured by the fluttering hen. He hopped closer, and again closer, until he was beside her. Then he hopped over to the other side of her. She turned towards him, they both stretched forward until their beaks touched, and we noticed that the cock was carrying a morsel of food which he put into the hen's beak.

The little scene was played out in a few minutes and the hen flew on to another tree with the cock following after. He started in flight with a few wing beats, and then came in to land with an elegant glide, a special gliding flight which these cocks only use in spring when they are courting a hen.

While we watched the two birds on this day they were never far apart. Sometimes, instead of cock following hen, the two flew together in a flying duet. Sometimes they stopped on a tree for a while, and sometimes we heard the singing of the blue tit's simple melody. A little later we saw them both together on an upright branch. The cock was above, the fluttering hen below. They touched beaks and the cock again fed the hen, this time with something looking like a bacon rind, perhaps from a neighbouring garden. The flying chases, the singing and the feedings were the blue tits' ways of courting each other. By spending so much time together over the weeks they grew to be familiar and easy with each other and became restless and uneasy when apart. The two birds were a 'winter couple' progressing towards spring, towards the time of the singing of the birds, which will be mating time.

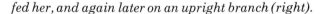

fed her, and again later on an upright branch (right).

When she vibrated her wings it was like a smile of encouragement...

Since we did not get to know this winter couple until February, we had to rely on our knowledge of other blue tits to imagine how our pair's own acquaintance had begun. They probably first found and favoured each other in mid-winter, or earlier. At this time they would have been living in a flock community with dozens of blue tits, great tits, and other small birds – many pairs of eyes searching for seeds and other winter foods, and carefully watching for clues from each other's success, as the days became shorter and colder, as supplies became scarce and survival chancy. During the hard winter months our pair may have begun to keep fairly close company within the flock and had their night roosts near to one another in the crevices of a usefully rotten old tree trunk. Before retiring in the early darkness of winter nights they would often have had a short flight together. Sometimes the cock may have accompanied the hen to her roost to sing briefly – a thin melody, nothing like his fuller song of spring – before retiring to his neighbouring nook.

As the days began to get steadily longer in January and February we knew that an important seasonal change was happening inside the birds' bodies. Small amounts of powerful chemical substances, the sex hormones, were being produced by special glands and released into the blood stream. These hormones started off great development in the reproductive organs: the hen's ovary for eggs to grow, and the cock's two testicles for sperm to be produced. However, eggs and sperm were not going to be ready until later in the season when the ovary and testicles had reached full development so that the birds became sexually mature.

The influence of longer daylight triggered this development, and food, warmth of weather and sunshine also played a continuous part. Yet not much would have come of it without the two birds' effect upon one another. The hormone boost to the development of reproductive organs led to a change in the birds' behaviour, only slight at first – a little extra interest shown in the opposite sex, a change of voice. Our birds, especially the cock, began to sing more, and with more melody. The hen led the cock a flying chase but made sure that she did not lose him. She vibrated her wings, and the effect of it was like a smile of encouragement. These were the outward signs of the sexual development taking place within the birds. All blue tits have the same pattern of such outward signs to which only a blue tit, and no other bird, will respond. But they are not robots going through fixed motions. Each individual blue tit has its own style, its own way of expression which clearly conveys 'I am me, distinct from all others'. It also says, 'I am a hen . . . I am a cock . . . I feel friendly.' Such encouraging responses made each bird even more interested in the other. This promoted further sexual development in both of them and that, in turn, stepped up the interest which kept them close to one another. The effect was like a game of leap-frog between hormones and behaviour where each in turn went ahead.

Our cock and hen needed one another to come to full sexual development. This is not true of all animals. Some mature first and meet later. For some, their time together is only a very brief business, for others a main part of their lives. Whichever it is, there is generally an ordered sequence for coming together which starts with a first tentative approach and leads step by step to mating. For our cock and hen the beginning had to be a careful acquaintance, moving on to something like friendship, and only gradually to a much closer bond, which between blue tits may then last for as long as both live. This is called a 'pair bond'. The bond works as if there were an invisible rubber band which can stretch to allow a pair to be apart for a while, but always draws them back together again. Many different animal couples form such a bond, and of course we see it also in people. It is not yet fully understood and is a very important subject of study at present. We do know that all species who form pair bonds have one thing in common: both partners collaborate later in rearing their young. The pair bond helps to ensure this. It is therefore found most strongly in those animals whose young are born helpless and in need of the kind of protection which, for best success, requires the care of two parents working together in close cooperation.

. . . he conveyed, 'I am a cock . . . I feel friendly.'

The 'landowner' surveying all in sight...

To become successful parents our pair had to find each other and they also had to find the surroundings, the environment, likely to provide the right food and shelter for their young. Their inclination to go and look for such a place came at the same time as their increased interest in the opposite sex. For some animals, like seals, or seagulls, this inclination takes them to densely populated summer breeding colonies. Others, like our birds, want just the opposite. They left the winter flock to strike out on their own.

Our blue tit pair were looking for what might be called a small insect farm of their own. They required trees and shrubs. A small garden would have done, but open woodland like ours would be preferred. Here they eventually established about two acres as their own, their so-called territory. From other studies we could assume that they knew the boundaries of their intended land claim, and were probably making regular flying patrols round these borders to keep an eye on all who passed. The increasing sexual development which had made them want to come here also made them much more vigilant. It particularly made the cock more alert to looking after hen and territory. By March we often found him sitting high, surveying all in sight, as any watchful landowner might. He would do this particularly near his boundaries, and also if he lost sight of the hen. He would call or sing and not rest until she came flying in from wherever she had been. His song attracted her, as her twittering also attracted him so that he would at other times fly over to her.

16

The usefulness of their song was not only for each other. It would be understood by other birds as information about our birds' identity and intentions. To other blue tits and all those who might be direct competitors for food, nest site, or mate, the message meant 'keep off . . . I am here . . . this area is already occupied'. However, blackbirds, robins and others who presented no threat of direct rivalry did not worry our pair and with these they shared their territory peacefully. Therefore we had many different kinds of birds around us, but a limited number of any one kind. They all sang, particularly in the dawn chorus and near sundown, each proclaiming its territory, each conveying to outsiders, 'I am here . . . if you are my own kind, go away.'

When we saw our cock one day sitting on a branch with crest feathers raised and all feathers puffed out, sounding a *drrrt . . . drrrt . . . drrrt* call, this showed that an unwelcome rival was in sight. It was a perfect picture of ruffled feelings. It made him appear pompous and bigger, quite as any warrior in a fighting mood might look. He would never rush into a fight, but nevertheless firmly showed that he was not inclined to back down. This was instantly understood by the intruder who respected the message and flew away. He might come back repeatedly to test our cock's persistence, but 'flight not fight' describes the rule for intruding birds in the face of opposition. Physical combat is altogether very rare in birds; it is all done by feathery and often noisy displays of intentions and threats, which are respected. In this, opponents can be quite determined and aggressive, yet without coming to physical blows upon one another. Thus birds in their graceful ways have shared out their living space for more than 100 million years.

The bad news from the cock to his rival was good news to us. It showed that he was becoming a successfully mature male, and that he was determined to stay. He had come to regard our land as his property.

. . . the 'warrior' puffing out his feathers.

She watched from a tree . . .

he pointed to the nest hole . . .

A Place to Nest

The nestbox on our window drew the birds' interest from the beginning. When they first came to our territory in late winter we used to find them gazing down at it from the safe distance of the tree opposite us. Later on, the hen one day watched from the tree as the cock flew over. He landed on the perch, and took a good look in. Then he backed away so that his whole body from beak to tail was in line with the nest hole. This gave the hen a prominent view of his white cheek feathers, with the horizontal dark streak at his eye level looking very much like a pointer. This indeed is known to be one of the cock's main ways of pointing out a promising nest hole to his hen.

To do so is his natural habit, as it is for the male amongst most hole-nesting birds, and most have similarly prominent head markings. Also, cocks often do some attention-getting hammering around the nest hole with their beaks. Ours evidently did, because we could see the zig-zag dents he had made around the edge of the hole. Having done his pointing-out, the cock turned around on the perch to face the hen. He whirred his wings slightly and called *tsee, tsee, tsee, tsit!* This did the trick: the hen came over to the perch to have a look for herself. As she approached he flew off. They were not yet entirely comfortable so near to each other under such restricted conditions. As people cannot help blinking their eyes when something comes too close to their face, so birds automatically flick out their wings when too closely approached by another bird. Therefore all birds have within them a 'safe-distance' caution which keeps them out of reach of one another. While such physical caution prevents fights and injury at other times of year, it would make mating impossible. Our pair would gradually have to overcome this shyness.

18

For about eight weeks, from February till the beginning of April, we watched our birds in their daily inspections of our nestbox. They had to rely on their sharp vision and hearing and their ability to get a general 'feel' of it. (Smell hardly came into it because birds, unlike mammals, have a very poor sense of smell.) Cock and hen came at all hours of the day. They came in sunshine, they came in dripping rain. This probably gave them important clues about the box's reliability, including exposure to wind, rain and dampness, or to sun and possible overheating. Again and again we found one of them peering into the entrance hole, looking up under the eaves, examining the box from all angles and hopping all over the roof. So far so good. Our box seemed to satisfy them. But they undoubtedly also regularly inspected other possible nesting sites which they would have turned to if they had found something wrong with ours.

Their final selection would be based on a wide knowledge of what was available in their territory. They probably had a passing acquaintance with nearly every nook and cranny in it. For hole-nesting birds this kind of inquisitiveness is an important part of routine explorations all through the winter. The search had become more serious when our landlord-cock had come to take a closer look at our box and had pointed it out to the hen. No doubt he had done the same at several other openings. Only certain ones would have attracted him. They might have been in trees, in old crumbling walls, or a tin can, or man-made nesting box. Wherever it was, his preference would be for a hole five feet or more above the ground, and with an opening no larger than a ten-pence piece. Better a tight fit than too large an entrance – a useful natural preference which ruled out hopeless competition with somewhat bigger hole-nesting birds such as sparrows or great tits. It also made it harder for predators, such as cats, to reach in.

. . . then faced her, whirred his wings and called.

Daily inspections from the outside to look up, and down, and over the roof.

The satisfactorily small opening had to lead into a cavity, unoccupied of course, and of reasonable size. It had to be bigger than a single-bird sleeping roost, but preferably not larger than our nestbox which had walls slightly smaller than the size of the pages of this book. The interior had to be snug and dry, and it was advantageous to find an entrance well above the floor – better for keeping out wind, rain and enemies. By nature the cock had a knack for recognizing the right kind of place, and we had made one for him. Still we could not be sure that our birds would stay. When it comes to making their choice the cock merely suggests; the hen finally selects.

Towards the end of March we felt that the birds had become sufficiently attached to the box and accustomed to our quiet presence, so that we would not frighten them off by taking the first photographs of the hen inside. We had already been able to see her there by the light coming in through the nest hole, and we knew she was occasionally staying overnight because sometimes we found additional bird droppings on the floor early in the morning. But while the natural light was enough for us to see, we needed to use photo-flash to illuminate the box for photography. A side effect of this was that the brightness of the flash blotted out the softer light coming in from outside, and this sometimes made the nest hole appear nearly black in the photographs. It looked particularly dark on this day because it was raining and grey outside. Our first portrait of the hen visiting her future nesting place caught her arriving dripping wet and be-draggled, as she came in out of a downpour to find the nestbox nice and dry. A double test was passed: the hen found the box weatherproof and we found that the hen accepted the brief flash of our light and was not frightened away.

20

The wet hen (below) came in out of the rain – our first photograph of her in the nestbox.

It was now March 31st and the hen was spending an increasing number of hours each day inside the nestbox. The cock was usually in close attendance near by and the two kept in touch calling *tsee, tsee, tsee, tsit*, back and forth. The hen had a regular round of activities which kept her steadily occupied. Coming in from outside she would usually begin by firmly pecking the floor. The noise of this hammering may have been an important indication to the cock that she approved of the box. The hen concentrated her pecking around one particular corner and this turned out to be where she later built the cup of her soft nest. Although the hammering merely pock-marked our hardwood floor, it could be a most productive habit to carve out a bigger hollow in nature's less spacious accommodations in the crumbly wood of an old tree. And if that happened

Acrobatic pecking at the hole . . .   *a session of floor hammering . . .*   *make-believe nest-making . . .*

to cause a rotten floor to collapse altogether it would be a great advantage to discover the weakness now. After a session of hammering the hen flopped down on the floor, and in a wiggling movement rubbed her breast over the wood while gently beating her outspread wings on it. It was like make-believe nest-making. Eventually those same movements will shape the real cup of her nest out of the building materials she will bring in. After these attentions to the floor the hen usually turned to the nest hole where she spent a lot of her time. Hanging on to it in a variety of acrobatic positions she pecked and scraped at it with her beak. This also could have been a useful part of her behaviour on softer wood, to make too small a hole larger, or to smooth off a rough one. In our box she achieved little but perhaps her efforts, and also the dents made by the cock's pecking from outside, had some meaning. Perhaps it was like carving one's initials on a tree; perhaps it was their way of putting their mark on it.

The hen looked to be well on the way to feeling at home in our box. One day in the midst of her domestic activities, she stopped abruptly. The gentle-looking hen was suddenly transformed into a fierce creature, with wing and tail feathers raised like spikes and a hissing sound coming from her open beak. In that instant the face of another blue tit appeared at the nest hole, peered in, and in a flash had gone again. Evidently this had been a stranger, perhaps another cock prospecting for a nest site. He quickly understood the unfriendly display, just as others had previously respected the puffed-up warrior cock's determination.

Once again the bad news to the intruder was welcome to us. The hen had conveyed 'I am here to stay'. This was no longer our box, it had become hers.

. . . unfriendly display to a stranger at the nest hole.

But still the nestbox remained empty. The hen kept up her domestic activities day after day with little to show for her efforts. She was in no hurry. Her first eggs would not be laid until the end of April, nearly a month away. Meanwhile, for shelter our pair needed nothing more than their neighbouring nooks in a tree. In fact, the cock never did move into the nest; he always camped out near by. Yet it was he who had originally taken the lead to search for a site and, in the two months since then, he and the hen had devoted at least as much time to the nesting site as to one another in courtship flights and feedings. What made them prepare for parenthood so well, and so well in advance? After all, they had no way of knowing that their courtship would lead to becoming parents. No one to tell them, no one to show them how.

The key to it was that in becoming sexually mature their interests changed altogether. Their interest in one another became intensified, and their feelings altered about what they wanted to do and where they wanted to be. Sexual development changed them in many ways, all of them in the direction of becoming parents. While their bodies developed towards producing eggs and sperm, the behaviour to go with these developed also. The function of eggs and sperm is to maintain the continuity of life from one generation to the next; the function of the accompanying behaviour is the same. Through this, our pair had a well-coordinated programme to provide what their hatchlings will need. There was no magic foresight in it, hen and cock simply followed what came naturally. Being free as a bird, meant being free to follow such very reliable natural feelings.

Finding a suitable place to nest is not always easy. There are usually more hole-nesting birds looking, than places to be found. It is therefore best to be early birds like ours, and for the hen to become a sitting tenant in a good place as soon as she has found one. Thus her activities now, even the urge for the make-believe nest-cupping, were not wasted effort. They tied her to the site, which helped to guard it against rivals, while the eggs inside her body were still microscopically small, and while the box remained bare and empty. It was a time of waiting. The waiting hen heard the cock calling outside. She drew herself up alertly and flew out to him, out among the trees which were still as bare and grey as the nestbox. That was the cause of the waiting.

The floor-pecking hen ... when the cock called (opposite) she drew herself up – to the height of the nail fixing the outside perch to the box.

APRIL

Spring Comes

During the first two weeks in April the view from our window became transformed: 'for lo, the winter is past . . . the flowers appear on the earth, and the time of the singing of the birds has come . . .' So say the lines from the Bible's *Song of Songs*, telling us that it has been the same for thousands of years and that animals, trees and flowers have been linked together in their life cycles through the ages.

In all those parts of the world where the seasons change, animal life is adapted accordingly. Animals mate at such a time that their offspring are born at the season which is most favourable for the survival of the young. Usually warm weather and plentiful food are the essentials. But neither of these comes at exactly the same time from year to year. Sometimes we have an early spring, sometimes a late one; and in southern parts of the country it is always earlier than further north. How do animals adjust to this from year to year, and according to a different schedule in different regions? A difficult question, especially when we know that new life cannot be instantly ready on the first good day. It takes a fixed amount of time for each kind of animal to be ready to hatch, or be born. Therefore, something connected with the seasonal change in the world around them must somehow give the parent animals advance notice to 'go ahead'; must somehow switch their interests to the particular activities which lead them step by step to parenthood.

When we saw our cock on the small apple tree opposite us, picking his way along a branch and intently examining the newly opened buds, we knew he was looking for food. Occasionally he would expertly jab his beak into a bud and nibble on what he had found. This was a new treat, not available until now. The opening tree buds contained the first tiny insect larvae to hatch this season. Hatching when the tender buds opened was the key to survival for the larvae; being found by a bird put an end to that insect's life, but was an important step towards new bird life. The new food, together with the other signs of spring, gave the advance notice our hen and cock needed, and were perceived by them as a go-ahead signal to advance to the next steps in their courtship.

27

The cock examined the newly opened buds.

On the fine morning of April 13th our cock took a big step ahead. This was the first time we saw him come to visit the hen in the empty box. He had just found a small insect larva and he came carrying it in his beak, and announced his approach with a soft greeting call. The hen heard it and when the cock stopped on the perch to look in, she stood ready to greet him. In contrast to the fierce reception she had given earlier to a stranger *(page 23)* she faced her mate meekly, with her wings tightly folded to her sides, her tail down, and her whole body looking as small as possible. She looked utterly harmless. The cock turned his head this way and that, and gave the impression of being torn between wanting to come in and being afraid to enter. The hen finally won him over when she began to make cheeping food-begging noises, sounding like a baby bird. This was irresistible to the cock and he hopped in, but shyly kept to the furthest wall, as close to the entrance and as far from the hen as possible. Quickly, he put the insect into her beak and in less than two seconds he was out and gone again.

In the brief visit cock, hen and insect had been brought together under one roof. It was like a check point where pair bond, new food and nest site were jointly confirmed. In spite of his first hasty exit, the cock came back several times that morning to bring the hen more insects and each time he received the same encouraging welcome. It was probably this which drew him back again and again. Each time he seemed less hesitant than before and more at ease in the nestbox. Different couples may come to this check point in different ways. Some cocks remain much more shy than ours and do not enter the nesting site at all at this stage; they call the hen out to feed her at the entrance hole, or near by. Each bird pair must find their way to communicate to each other repeated reassurances that the pair bond is holding, that insects are now hatching, and that they continue to have a satisfactory nesting site. We can be sure that such check-point communication must take place, otherwise we would find birds barging ahead to breed helter skelter, with or without a pair bond, with or without a place to nest, mating and producing eggs at unpredictable seasons and in unsuitable places. They don't, because they cannot go ahead until their reactions tell them to, and their reactions come out only when the right conditions come together.

He arrived (opposite) for his first feeding visit.

Her first straw barred her entry . . .

We watched hen and cock closely for the rest of that day. In mid-afternoon the hen flew out as she usually did for a meal or a flight with the cock. She disappeared from our sight for a while and returned carrying a large piece of straw. We had never before seen her bringing anything back to the box. She may never have done it in her life before. Although straw could have been found all along, she had not been inclined until this afternoon to search for it, pick it up, and try to carry it into her box. There she came up against a problem: her entry was barred by the straw she was carrying crosswise. She gave up and took the straw away again. Soon she was back with another stalk even bulkier than the first but this time, by luck or learning, the straw was aimed in the right direction and she managed to thread it through the nest hole and struggled in with it.

How did she know what to look for and what to do with it? She had no example to copy, no instructions given to her. She had only her own inner 'instructions' which came into action on this day when the cock first fed her in the nestbox. It gave her a craving for something other than food. Only something which looked and felt like a piece of nest-building material could satisfy the craving. To come to feel like that and also to be able to take the right action was as much a part of her as, for instance, wanting to fly and also being able to fly. The hen who had inherited the shape of her body, wings and feathers from her parents also inherited the pattern of her actions from them, such as flying in a certain way – and nest-building in a certain way. These actions are called inborn, or innate, behaviours because they are inherited and need not be learned. Inborn behaviour develops and grows up along with the body. When our two birds explored crevices in trees during the winter, this was inborn behaviour. When the cock pointed out a good nest site to the hen he did it in the inborn manner, which all blue tits have in common. Now the hen's nest-building followed a basically inborn pattern.

30

The lives of our two birds were largely organized by inborn behaviour. This was not like a long-playing record which played itself out from beginning to end automatically. Inborn behaviour is made up of separate steps of behaviour which follow one after another in a definite sequence, but not automatically. Each step followed only when 'switched on' by exact combinations of influences. These influences were of two kinds, internal and external. The internal ones originated within the birds. An empty stomach gave them an interest in food. Increased production of sex hormones made the opposite sex more attractive and turned their activities towards parenthood. However, these internal influences were often strongly affected by preceding external events. External influences all came directly from outside and were the combined effects of everything the birds perceived in their environment, including longer daylight, the weather, food supplies, finding a nestbox, and also many social effects such as the attentions one bird received from the other.

. . . she managed to struggle in on the next attempt.

Getting her aim right ... but not yet her landing (opposite).

On this day the sun was shining, the cock had come to feed the hen in the nestbox, and since her hormones had made her ready within herself, the whole combination brought out her inborn urge to want something of a certain kind. She was moved to fly out in search of satisfaction. The sight of straw fitted the picture of what she wanted. She stopped to pick it up and took it back to the nestbox. That made up a three-step unit of behaviour for nest-building: searching, picking up, carrying back to the nest. The three steps followed each other in an orderly and effective sequence. Such linking of single acts also appears to be inherited as a kind of package unit, so that going out to search, and finding what she wanted, then brought the hen back to the nest with the straw. She did not stop midway with the straw to wonder what to do with it.

Being born able to build a nest did not mean our hen was fully expert at it from the start. Experience helped and she soon improved in aiming her straws into the nest hole. But when she ambitiously trailed in a particularly long piece, she lost her balance and nearly fell over backwards – a beginner's bad landing!

After a few collecting trips, at first for straw and then for moss, the hen always stayed in the box for a while and returned to her familiar housekeeping activities. She pecked around her chosen corner and wiggled and fluttered over the floor with nest-cupping movements which were still only make-believe. The nest-cupping was linked to the collecting steps. Two or three collecting trips satisfied that urge and led to the urge for a session of nest-making inside the box. A spell of this, plus feeding visits from the cock, then stirred up a renewed impulse to go out and collect again, which led back to nest-making again. Such an orderly, largely inborn, set of action patterns alternating between collecting and nest-making will eventually get the job done.

The cock did not participate in nest-building. For him it was not inborn to do so. This is usually true of all the cocks of his kind, but not true among all birds. Some male birds help, and some even do all of the nest-building. However, our cock was not just an idle bystander. He had after all originally been the main nest finder. Now he was chief insect gatherer and he also vigilantly watched over the nestbox and the hen. While she was busy inside, he continued to stay in the vicinity and kept in touch with her by regularly sounding his greeting call and bringing her food.

Back to housekeeping, she wiggled and fluttered over the floor.

When the hen was in the mood for a break she flew out to join him. In the late afternoon they nibbled grubs on our hawthorn tree, he above and she below. For a while the nestbox seemed forgotten. Shortly after eight o'clock in the evening the hen came back. Up till now she had usually stayed out overnight but after this first day of building she took to sleeping in the nestbox each night, and the cock roosted alone outside – yet always within calling distance.

Look-out stop before entering.

Busy Building

The third day of building began quietly. We found the hen sitting in her corner, feet tucked under, and looking around brightly as if taking stock. In the past two days she had piled bunches of moss on top of the straw and a small piece of string had also taken her fancy. Her arrangements were casual but tidy. All the material was placed against the two walls of the box opposite the favourite corner which was still kept clear, except for one stray sprig of moss.

All along the hen had chosen to favour a corner of the box which was as hidden and protected as possible from the outside world. It will be the safest place in the nest for her eggs and later for her defenceless brood. But while we were able to look forward to eggs and brood, the hen herself had no way of knowing such future events. Nevertheless, it was not surprising that it was inborn to her to make such a forward-looking choice. This is easiest to understand if one thinks backwards. Our hen would not have had much chance to grow up if her parents had not made the right provisions for their young. The same was true of their parents, and all the way back down the line. Our hen and cock owed their lives to the fact that each of their ancestors had safely and successfully raised a family, and through this had passed on their inheritance. The inherited behaviour which leads to parenthood is particularly important because this creates the next generation, and the next, and the next . . . keeping the chain of life going as each set of parents dies. Without reliable behaviour in reproduction no species can survive in the long run.

After a brief rest in her corner the hen flew away. She reappeared outside with a beakful of moss and landed on a budding tree overlooking our window. She leaned down to observe the nestbox and then flew nearer to land on a log which stood on the roof of a shed only a few feet from our window. From there she had a very close view of her home. It had become her habit to make these look-out stops before entering. She

Expertly zooming in like a bullet . . . and (below) rescuing an off-balance entry.

turned her head in all directions to look around and again gazed particularly at her nest site. If she had seen anything amiss or strange she would not have approached. Her inclination for such caution would warn her of any signs of danger in the box. It would also help prevent leading invaders to her secret hideaway. Since the coast was clear, the hen swooped over and straight into the nest hole without using the perch. Three days of practice had impressively improved her skill. No longer awkwardly struggling in, she came zooming in like a bullet. Another time she was able to rescue an off-balance entry by quickly flipping out one wing, as she extended her landing-gear feet for a smooth touchdown.

Belly flop nest-making . . . and (below) flutter-beating the moss.

The hen put down her newly collected moss, picked it up again, put it somewhere else, and fussed over it until she was satisfied. In the usual pattern the urge then swept over her to get down in a belly flop for some nest-making. She pushed her feet against the wall and performed her nest-cupping wiggle over the corner of the floor which she still kept clear. When she swung around and spread her wings she at last had some material to work with, and the activity was no longer entirely make-believe. Her choice of moss as a building material fitted together with the particular flutter-beating motion of her wings. This matted the moss down to knit the pieces together. With more and more moss it will gradually become like a springy mattress.

Having spent three days on such a promising start in accumulating moss, the hen suddenly went into reverse. She switched to collecting moss *from* the nest and carried it *out*, and away. This was new. Had she become confused? Or was some of the moss not to her liking – was she exchanging it for something better? She carried on like this for the next two days going in both directions, carrying moss in, and carrying so much out again, that the nestbox continuously lost as much as it was gaining. The hen was steadily busy, without getting anywhere. It reminded us of a housewife moving the furniture here and there and back again, busily attached to her house without adding to its contents. It reminded us, too, of the hen's earlier activities in the empty box.

Why was she collecting moss from the nest ...

. . . and carrying it out and away?

Indeed, the weather had turned cool again, as it had been then. The cock too changed his ways. He hardly came to the nestbox and we only rarely saw him feeding the hen during these two days. The progress of spring had temporarily come to a halt, and apparently so did the progress in courtship and nest-making. Since the hen had switched to moss-carrying, it was not wasted effort to carry on with this, without going ahead for a while. It kept her tied to the right activity, tied in her interests to the nest, and ready to sprint to the finish any day, as soon as her sensitive inborn perceptions gave her the go-ahead again.

Our hen probably could have finished her nest in about three straight working days. Some hens do it all in one such sprint, while others dawdle over the task for as long as a month. The ones who take longest are those who are fortunate to find and take possession of a desirable nesting site early in the season, as our birds did. This enabled the hen to get off the mark in building at the very first signs of insect-hatching. If it had turned out to be a truly early and insect-rich spring, this would have given our pair a head start in getting the richest pickings for their young at the peak of the insect harvest. However, the first warm spell turned out to be a false promise followed by a return of cooler weather, which would bring a slowing down of the insect hatch. Therefore it was good that our hen matched this with a slow-down in nest-making, yet without losing interest or leaving her box unguarded.

On April 18th, after the three-day slow-down, sun and warmth returned and the cock's feeding visits picked up again. On that day the hen brought in a lot of moss and took out only a little. After that she never again carried out any of it.

The cock always announced his arrival with a greeting call just before he touched down on the perch outside the box. He never took to the hen's custom of zooming straight in and always stopped at the entrance to look in first. The hen, having recognized the sounds of his approach, stood ready to greet him by the time his face appeared at the nest hole. Through time and experience her greetings had become much more elaborate with much baby-bird twittering, with her tail swept low and slightly fanned, with her wings laid elegantly back. All her defences were down but she no longer looked as insignificant as she had when the cock first visited her. Now she looked more grand and quite at ease in her encouragements to the cock. He no longer showed any hesitation and entered as soon as he caught sight of the twittering hen. He showed that he came in peace by the way his feathers were smoothly flattened down, so flat that he looked almost like a wingless, tail-less bird as he leaned forward to feed the hen. He still looked rather shy, not so much at home in the nest as she. He fed her and within a few seconds always made a quick escape. Yet in about ten or fifteen minutes he was usually back, and the whole greeting and feeding ceremony was repeated, again and again. The hen's eager greeting displays encouraged him to bring more food, and that prompted her to build more.

The repeated feeding feasts were not only an incentive to building. They accomplished a great deal more because the particular nutritional values of caterpillars were essential. The birds' taste for caterpillars was not accidental, it was related to the hen's need for them. Caterpillars, from which moths and butterflies would grow, contain the right balance of protein-rich food which the hen required so that her body could produce nutritious eggs, from which chicks could grow.

In addition, the division of labour between cock and hen was useful in maintaining constant links between the two birds, and between them and their environment. Since the cock's programme kept him outdoors looking for caterpillars to bring to the hen, he served as a link between her and the outside world. The number of his visits, and the amount of food he brought, were like a continuous food and weather report for her, which affected her building programme. The fact that the hen was so dependent on the cock, instead of searching for her own food, had further great advantages. It left her free to concentrate on nest matters and, above all, it had the effect of making sure that the two birds kept in close touch with one another. It kept each bird well informed about the intentions and welfare of its mate. If one of them had met an accident, or lost interest, the other would soon have known. Since all was well with our birds, each twittering encounter reinforced the couple's pair bond and their desire to go on.

The greeting and feeding ceremony
was repeated again and again.

42

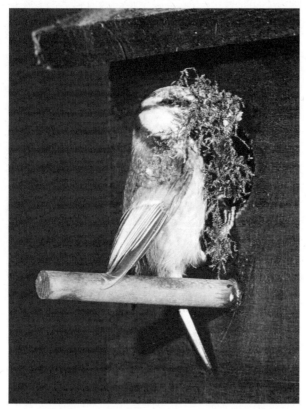

On the next day, April 19th, the hen seemed charged with new energy and really got going. In two busy building days she finished the bulk of her nest. No more dainty bunches of moss now. She turned up with great loads nearly as large as herself and stuffed herself through the nest hole with them. As the moss and a little additional straw piled up all around, it all looked in a great muddle. The hen rushed to and fro. But after every few collecting trips she dug into the moss with an apparent plan to get it sorted out, and we watched how she did it.

Within a few hours the floor of her favourite corner was covered over. When she dived in for nest-cupping stints she was nearly submerged as she pushed her feet against the wall and wiggled her whole body, and did her best to flutter-beat her wings against the welter of moss. Gradually it all became matted down to form a more or less evenly thick mattress reaching nearly to the height of the nailhead which fixed the outside perch to the box. That was as high as the hen's head had reached when she stretched up during the days of waiting in the empty box *(page 25)*.

What a muddle! ...

digging in to sort it out ...

nearly submerged ...

finally, moss up to the nailhead.

Her usual look-out stop.

On the sunny afternoon of April 20th we were looking towards the roof of our shed where the hen usually made her look-out stops before entering the nest. When she arrived she was carrying a beakful of fine smooth grasses and no moss. We had expected that this change from rough to smooth materials would happen soon. We knew that, at this stage of near completion of the nest, the downy feathers of the hen's underbelly were dropping out bit by bit, and the skin of her belly was becoming naked and altogether a lot more sensitive to anything touching it. It made her a lot more fussy about what she wanted to lie down on. The loss of her belly feathers was caused by an increase in reproductive hormones circulating in her blood; the same hormones that also promoted the formation of eggs in her ovary. Through the internal action of these hormones, the ripening of eggs and the loss of feathers happened simultaneously – eggs and bare underbelly were bound to go together. The denuded belly was the so-called brood patch. Only such featherless skin could provide a sufficient degree of heat for incubating eggs. The eggs, and later the delicate hatchlings, would profit directly from the protection of the soft lining which the hen was starting to bring in now. Thus, her hormones, the brood patch, and the softer nesting material were all preparations for the future. While the hen was simply making herself more comfortable for the moment, she was in fact working towards the better survival of her chicks.

The hen brought the fine grasses in and placed them over the moss in her special corner. She settled down in it and wiggled about in a nest-cupping way. But then, instead of going on, she puffed out her feathers, tucked her head under her wing and curled up for an afternoon nap. The hen who had looked so bright sitting in the half-empty nest five days ago *(page 36)* was tired out now and in need of a rest. After ten minutes she awoke and went on with her work until about half past eight in the evening.

Afternoon nap.

Protected in her cosy corner.

Fur, Feathers and Mating

The hen completed her nest with a layer of fur and feathers. We could best see the downy fluffiness of it by the rays of daylight streaming in from outdoors through the nest hole. This natural lighting, without use of our photo-flash, enabled us to see the hen only dimly. It showed how well protected she was in the shaded hollow of the nest cup she had created. She had turned our bare and hard box into a soft and cosy world of her own.

When the hen had switched to searching for fine grasses we anticipated that the increasingly sensitive brood patch on her belly would next lead her to look for still softer materials like fur, feathers, or wool. Scraps of sheep wool would have appealed to her, or she might even have boldly flown up to a cow, or a horse, and plucked a few tufts right off its back. Hens like ours have been seen to do that and the animal donor did not seem to mind. To see how quick our hen would be at recognizing what she wanted, when she first wanted it, we placed a square of rabbit fur on the leafy ground within sight of our house. This was on April 22nd, when the hen had not yet brought in any fur. In less than an hour the patch of white fur had caught the hen's eye. She landed near to it and guardedly hopped closer, stopping several times to look carefully all around before she hopped right up to the fur. She pecked at it once or twice, and looked around again. Everything was quiet and calm. Then, as expertly as if she had done it all her life, she grabbed hold of the fur with her beak, firmly pulled out a few wads of it, and made several return trips back to the nest, each time bringing in as much as she could hold in her beak.

Finding fur on the ground.

She worked on the fur with her beak . . .   *then dived into the fluffy layer . . .*   ►

In a short while she accumulated a sizeable ball of rabbit fur in the nest. She set to work on it, using her beak like a needle, or crochet hook, to pick rapidly at the fur, and tuck it into the moss in her nest cup, while at the same time fluffing and spreading it out. Then she dived into the fluffy layer and with her nest-cupping wiggle, using feet and belly and wings, she gradually deepened a cup-shaped hollow. After working on the fur she flew out for fine grasses and intertwined these around the nest cup.

Following the hectic three-day rush to finish her moss-mattress, the hen's pace of work had become leisurely again. The bedding was quite good enough now for eggs, but none came while the hen fussed and fiddled over the finishing touches to her nest. She seemed to be in a waiting period once again, and again this came at the same time as a set-back in the weather. For five days it was grey and wet, and so chilly that we even had a flurry of snow on April 26th. Combined with this, as before during bad weather, the cock made only rare feeding visits to the nest. All around, the hen was exposed to evidence that the season had taken a bad turn. It was our pair's last chance for adjusting their breeding programme to the season. The cold weather, and lack of solicitous attentions and food from the cock, were probably having a combined effect to slightly delay the final ripening of the eggs in the hen's body.

She came with hair and more grasses . . .   *picked up her special feather . . .*   ►

plodded on through rain bringing soggy fur . . .

then made a circle of intertwined grasses.

Having come this far the hen did not disrupt her nest by carrying material in and out, as she had done during her earlier slow-down. She kept on with the work started, but made slow progress. She plodded on through the foul weather, collected soggy wet rabbit fur and came in with it, looking drenched herself. The next day was dry but still chilly. She brought in a white downy feather which she treated as a somewhat special prize. She put it to the front, then moved it to the back of the nest and went out. She returned with a mixture of grasses and fine badger hair, probably found near a badger set. She put these down amongst the moss, then picked up the white feather again and stood as if deliberating where to put it. Finally, she tucked it into the middle of her nest cup and sat down at the centre of her creation.

It is possible that the hen had a certain decorative sense in her art of nest-building, along with wanting to make it comfortable for herself. The immediate goal of her in-born behaviour had to be to please herself. She did not need to be able to contemplate the future. Sense of duty did not come into it. The future survival of her offspring totally depended on the fact that hen and cock, by nature, found all the preparations for parenthood what we, for ourselves, would call enjoyable or satisfying.

tucked it into the nest cup . . .

and sat down in the circle of grasses.

Before we were to see eggs, three events had to take place: ovulation, mating and fertilization. The first of these, ovulation (from the Latin word *ovum* meaning egg) was probably on its way right now within the hen's body, purely under the control of her hormones. In ovulation the ripened eggs burst from a hen's ovary (meaning egg-ary) and pass into her oviduct (egg-duct, or tube). Each of these eggs consists of an almost invisibly small living part, which bears all the inheritance from the hen, and this living dot is embedded on the food-rich yolk. One at a time is ovulated to start a four-day journey down within the oviduct. The oviduct is like a biological production line where first egg white and then shell become wrapped around the yolk.

Fertilization, like ovulation, is also an entirely internal event. It happens after mating, when the microscopically small sperm cells from the cock swim up on their own, high up into the hen's oviduct, and enter into her eggs before these have any egg white or shell around them. The sperm cells carry the cock's inheritance to be joined together with the hen's inheritance. Each of the eggs is fertilized by one sperm, and each new life gets an equal inheritance from both parents. But the combination of inheritance comes out differently in each fertilized egg so that each new bird will have its own individual characteristics, like brothers and sisters, not identical twins.

Mating is different from ovulation and fertilization because it is not just an internal process; it could not happen without cock and hen together taking specific action. Without this the cock's sperm would not get to the hen and there could be no chance for fertilization. The pattern for this behaviour is inborn, and a very strong urge has to go with it to overcome all other interests, or fears, so that the two birds utterly concentrate on one another, and with more intimacy than ever before.

On their way to mating, our hen and cock were on the branches of a rugged old tree. She spread her wings especially wide and fluttered them. He turned around and looked at her intently, then they flew off together into dense dark shrubbery where we could no longer photograph them. The hen again started up her wing vibrations, the cock too fluttered his wings slightly and both birds chirped in high-pitched tones which we had not heard before. Their twitterings and wing vibrations became more and more excited as the cock edged up close to the hen and then hopped on top of her, to stand on her back. In the same instant she raised her tail up so that her body opening, the cloaca, was exposed underneath the tail. The cock's body twisted downwards to bring his cloaca directly over hers. His cloaca was an opening exactly like the hen's because, unlike mammals, the males of most bird species do not have a penis. When we saw the cock perched like that on top of the hen and heard the rising sound of their twittering, we knew that in these moments of heightened excitement a stream of sperm-carrying fluids was flowing from the cock through his cloaca into the hen's. This led directly into her oviduct, enabling the sperms to swim up on their own.

The mating lasted only a few seconds. The cock hopped off the hen, the two birds fluffed out their feathers, chirped softly and then flew off together. They would mate again, perhaps a short while later, certainly numerous times in the days to come. They had not done so until the nest was ready and the season was right. Now they had the urge to mate frequently and this would help to ensure that all the eggs became fertilized.

Ten Speckled Eggs

On April 27th the hen nestled down for the night by half past seven in the evening, about an hour earlier than usual. On the following morning we heard the cock calling softly from outside where bright sun was filtering through the fresh green leaves of spring. The hen gave the cock an eager welcome but did not get up as always before. When she arched her back to reach up for his caterpillar we saw that there was one egg under her. When the cock flew out, the hen followed him, and her first speckled white egg was left alone on its bed of feathers.

Nestling down (opposite). Next day (above) the first egg shown at life size at right.

In ten days the hen laid ten eggs, one a day early each morning. As soon as the first egg was laid the hen totally changed her way of life. For weeks she had been spending nearly all of her time inside the nestbox; now she suddenly kept away from it during most of her waking hours and left her eggs deserted. She had not turned into a neglectful mother. Without the warmth of her body her newly laid eggs could survive for some time while their development was arrested in a so-called 'dormant' state, from the Latin word meaning sleep. The hen's overnight switch in behaviour benefitted her brood as a whole because she eventually incubated her eggs together, as one clutch, so that they became warmed up and started to grow together, to hatch near to the same day. For hens like ours, who often lay more than a dozen in one brood, the inborn 'delay switch' against immediate incubation prevents the first-laid from becoming too advanced over the others. Otherwise, the first two or three hatched would have such an age advantage in size and abilities that this would have ruined the chances of survival for the later younger ones. Nor would the lone survivors do very well, because they would then lack the cuddling warmth of nestmates close in age. Once again the hen's behaviour was forward-looking in its effects thanks to inborn reactions, largely under the influence of her hormones. Particular ones had reached their highest level which brought on egg-laying, with egg after egg going through the internal production line. The hen's body was geared entirely to this, and it made her want to be outside and gave her a huge appetite. To produce sufficiently food-rich eggs she required one-third more food each day than she normally needed.

Bringing more fluff . . .

. . . shuffling around.

56

Eggs exposed . . .   *eggs covered up again.*

She used her time outside mainly to gorge herself in teamwork with the cock: he fed her and she ate. During these days they took advantage of the tiniest grubs and insects which were particularly abundant right now, but were far too small to make transport to the nest worthwhile. The pair sat side by side on a branch. The cock busily snatched up grubs and with a turn of his head passed them into the hen's beak. When he had cleared everything edible within easy reach they moved on to the next good eating place with the hen giving the cock unfailing twittering and wing-fluttering encouragement.

Keeping away from the eggs did not keep the hen from showing keen interest in them. She came back to the nest for many brief visits all day long. She brought in more badger hair, fur and feathers, and worked these into the soft nest cover. She straddled the nest cup and shuffled around, and dug in for bouts of nest-cupping which usually brought the eggs to the surface. She would stand and gaze at them, then fuss and wiggle over them until the eggs disappeared again under the fluffy nest covering. She never left the eggs uncovered for more than a few moments and we rarely got to see them. Such concealment would be useful against any egg thief, such as a weasel or magpie who could reach in even through the small nest hole. The blanket would also be protection against any unseasonal cold. But the most important known value of this habit is not protection against cold but protection against warmth, the warmth of the hen's brood patch. The hen did occasionally sit over her eggs, and slept on them every night. The downy blanket insulated the eggs from the hen's hot brood patch so that they stayed dormant at an evenly cool temperature and were not exposed to on-again, off-again warming-up bouts.

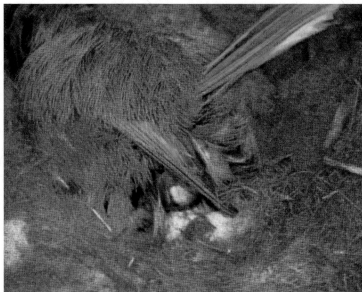

Eyes closed, tail up, cloaca stretching open . . .   *the egg soon appeared in the cloaca . . .*

We stayed up one night to watch the hen lay her daily egg which always arrived well before the bright light of day. From midnight on we looked in on her periodically by the light of a small torch. She slept soundly, curled up over her eggs. Shortly before five o'clock in the morning, when it was still dark with only a hint of light on the horizon, the birds outside were tuning up for the dawn chorus. The hen awoke and began to shuffle casually over the nest cup. But after a short while she became agitated and restless. She got up to look at her eggs. She turned some of them over with her beak and then went back to sit over them. The restlessness stopped. She did not move, closed her eyes, drew her head in, and looked tense and straining with effort. She opened her beak but made no sound; she panted for breath. At the same time her tail slowly went up and we saw that the cloaca under the tail was stretching wide open, and the white shell of an egg became visible in it. The egg was travelling down through the oviduct and was about to emerge from the same opening where the sperm had gone in at mating. Within half a minute the broad half of the egg was out and the rest slipped through in a few seconds. As the egg gently landed on top of the others the folds of the cloaca closed up again. The egg's broad end had acted as a wedge to open up the way, and the shell's smooth and streamlined surface made it possible for the egg to slide through easily. A square or knobbly egg would have given the hen an awful problem. As it was, it took altogether only a little over five minutes from the first uneasy restlessness until the egg was out. It had been a short but intense effort. The hen was exhausted by it and sat panting for another couple of minutes. Then she got up, fluffed out her feathers, and after covering up the latest egg she turned to fly out, probably for her breakfast with the cock.

58

it slid out broad end first . . .

and gently landed on top of the others.

After a brief rest the hen looked around brightly, then flew out.

She plunged straight in . . .   *to roll the eggs over . . .*   *revealing her naked brood patch.*

After the hen had laid her eighth egg a complete change came over her again. She gave up her feeding feasts with the cock outdoors and within the next two days – while she went on to lay eggs number nine and ten – she became a full-time nest-dweller again. Food lost its attractions; she now wanted to stay with her eggs. She stopped covering them up and they were exposed to the direct heat of her brood patch when she sat on them. It is thought that the feel of a certain bulk of eggs 'turns on' the hen's urge to brood, and that this then has an internal effect in the hen to 'turn off' further production of the hormones which brought on ovulation and laying. In this way the beginning of brooding would lead to the end of egg-laying.

The hen stuck to her brooding all day, in solid two-hour shifts with only five to ten minutes off outdoors in between. She never stayed out long enough for the eggs to be in any danger of cooling down too much. Upon her return from such outings she first of all plunged head down and turned her eggs over. She did this with her feet braced against the sides of the nest cup and used her closed beak to push the eggs and roll them over. She worked strenuously, holding her balance with her tail, straight up, or flipped right and left. The hen repeatedly turned her eggs about once every twenty minutes. Such turning is believed to aid their normal development, and in commercial chicken hatcheries eggs are also turned over in mechanized incubators, copying the hen's inborn behaviour.

60

When the hen turned her eggs we had a good view of her naked brood patch. The exposed skin looked inflamed and wrinkled because an increased network of blood vessels had developed in it and the skin had become thickened. The increased supply of the hen's warm blood made that skin dark red and hotter than usual. It was like a hot water bottle radiating a temperature of over one hundred degrees Fahrenheit, which is warmer than normal human skin temperature. The hen kept her hot-water-bottle brood patch so faithfully over the smooth round eggs because this felt good to her. She stayed settled in the nest simply because she felt best there at this stage.

However, settling down was hardly the word for brooding. The frisky hen was in motion all the time. She never seemed to have a dull moment, bustling and bobbing about, tossing feathers up in the air, shifting this way and that, as she rubbed her brood patch over the eggs. Her wiggling made the nest cup become so deep that she sometimes nearly disappeared into the downy fluff, although she was sitting on top of the mound of ten eggs. Her activeness may have been helpful to keep her fit. It may also have been important to keep air circulating around the eggs.

During the first ten brooding days, the cock had a rest. He came only rarely to the nest to feed the hen and only occasionally fed her outside during her brief excursions. This made sense since she no longer required extra food for producing eggs, and there was no longer any use for seasonal go-ahead or for go-slow signals. The eggs were launched, and growing according to their own time schedule to hatch in about two weeks. Until then all they needed was warmth. Four days before the two weeks were over, the cock's feeding visits began to pick up again and in two more days he was checking in with food every ten to fifteen minutes. It is possible that there was faint noise of activity coming from the nearly ready chicks within the eggs. We could not hear this, but it has been detected in many different kinds of eggs. The hen may have perceived it, and her behaviour may have changed towards the cock, which made him change. We could not tell what caused him to restart the feedings, but knew that it meant hatching was probably near.

Tossing feathers and wiggling over the eggs.

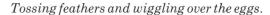

Seven Pink Blue Tits

On May 18th we had a proud family scene at our window when the cock came confidently flying in and the chirpy hen revealed one tiny pink chick under her, hatched from its egg early that morning.

The hen did not wait to be fed. She energetically rose up to meet the cock half way and we saw that in fact four very newly hatched tiny chicks had been lying under her. The hen took the caterpillar from the cock but did not eat it herself. The hatching of her chicks had such a strong effect on her that she did something quite new with the caterpillar. Instead of eating it herself she held it in her beak and leaned over the hatchlings with it. Along with that she also made a quite new sound, a soft evenly repeated *chirrup . . . chirrup*. The four droopy-looking pink bodies lay in a heap. Not a head stirred. The hen patiently stood over them and continued to chirp softly. At last two wobbly blind-eyed heads surfaced, and one of the small beaks opened. Seeing the chick's gaping beak made the hen deftly aim her own beak into it, and she released the caterpillar into the throat of the hatchling. It was a skilful reaction inborn to her and brought out by the way the chick looked and acted. The chick had played its part with equally effective

62

inborn ability. It had hatched from its egg able to respond by raising its head and opening its beak gapingly wide when hungry. The helpless, blind and naked new hatchlings had the one asset for survival which any newborn needs: they had parents attracted by their own offspring, who were lying there each occasionally offering up a small gaping mouth.

There is a great difference in abilities at birth among different kinds of animals. Many are at first very helpless, and often blind, like our birds. Kittens and puppies are like that. They cannot move around very much and totally depend on a parent who comes to them and looks after them. On the other hand, there are many other kinds of animals such as ducks, domestic chickens, calves, lambs and foals, which are much more advanced by the time they are born. They come out with open eyes and are quickly able to walk, even run, and follow their mothers around. The human baby is special because it is very helpless and cannot walk at birth, yet its eyes are already open and its senses are well developed from the start. What counts is not how helpless an animal is at birth; the only thing that really matters is that parents and young tend to be so well adapted to one another.

She took the caterpillar . . .

and put it into the small gaping beak.

Pulling at the stringy yolk . . .

nibbling egg shells . . .

The helpless-looking hatchlings had to be just strong enough to do one first thing for themselves: they broke out of their egg shells without any assistance from the hen. A fifth young joined the first four later on the same day, and number six struggled out of its shell the next morning. The hen was standing by and noticed some egg remnants on the head of the latest newcomer. She tried to pick it clean. It was dried yolk which stuck fast and was so stringy that the little head was pulled up high along with it. With persistence, and without injuring the chick, the hen finally succeeded and ate up the bit of egg leftovers. She also nibbled the discarded shells which contained calcium and other substances to make them hard. These were the same ingredients needed to keep the hen's bones, beak and claws hard.

The seventh young hatched two days after the first and that completed the family. The three remaining eggs never came to life; something must have gone wrong in their development. The hen paid them no particular attention and they stayed unbroken in the nest to the end. From now on the new hatchlings constantly engaged her interest. She watched over them, and fed them very frequently because the cock also was so aroused by the new situation that he more than doubled his efforts. We could rarely count more than three or four minutes between his arrivals with caterpillars which he gave to the hen and she always gave to the young. Together the chicks got at least 600 feedings a day, and without this amount of food all seven could not have survived. In these first few days they would also certainly have died without their hot-water-bottle mother. Their dependence on her warmth was matched by the fact that her brood patch remained bare for a few more days, and the hen regularly spread herself over her brood.

In between feedings she wiggled and bobbed about on top of the hatchlings exactly as she had on the eggs. And, as before in egg-turning, she plunged in often and gave the young quite a tossing which sent one up into the air along with a never-hatched egg *(opposite)*. The hatchlings came to no harm, and may have benefitted from the exercise, especially the youngest and weakest, who otherwise might have sunk to the bottom of the pile. Also, like the shaking out of any downy blanket, this tossing helped to

calling to greet the cock as she watched her young . . .

keep the nest material fluffed up for better warmth insulation. After the shuffling sessions the hen plunged head-down deeper where she would remove any litter she found, perhaps bits of shell, or any lice or other parasite pests. Such an inborn routine for keeping the nest clean was essential to the healthy survival of the brood.

The hen was so occupied with her chicks that the cock could no longer count on twittering welcomes. On the fourth day he was faced merely by the busy hen's up-ended tail, and waited until she briefly raised her head to receive his caterpillar. Meanwhile, a tiny head had popped up in the corner, a small beak opened up signalling 'look at me . . . feed me!' This told us that the chicks were growing up and were about to take a more active part in life.

spreading herself over her brood . . .

tossing the chicks and an egg.

A tiny head (far left) signalled 'feed me!'

65

She plunged her beak in . . .   *and left the green grub in the open mouth.*

After four days the new birds became more expert in gaping for food and needed no more coaxing. This one had detected the vibration of the cock's landing in the nest and popped straight up before the hen started to chirp. The orange colour of the hatchling's mouth, framed by its bright yellow beak-flange, stood out like a raised flag in the dim light of the nest. It presented an irresistible target for the hen to gently plunge her beak in. The tiny mouth opened up so wide that the hen's whole beak disappeared into it and she released the caterpillar far enough down to be easily swallowed. We could see the tail-end of the green caterpillar in the open mouth and then watched the progress of its green colour shimmering through the delicate skin of the chick's remarkably long neck – the longer, the better for getting the mouth up to be seen and fed.

One chick was satisfied and dropped off to sleep and out of sight. Four others stood ready and waiting when the next caterpillar arrived. An empty stomach made each chick alert to the sounds and vibrations connected with a parent bringing food. Their inborn behaviour went into action: heads were blindly raised, straight up in line

Going down, the green grub showed through the chick's throat.

Competing mouths waiting for food.

against gravity, and with no ability as yet to point towards the parent. At the same time their mouths gaped wide open. This gaping happens automatically in response to the parents' arrival, just as a hungry kitten, or indeed a human baby, sucks when a teat is put in its mouth.

When the hen was faced with the four competing mouths she hesitated a few seconds until she singled out the one which most drew her attention, and fed it. The others got their chance on the next round. After each feeding the hen would stand and watch the young for a few more seconds. As a result she was bound to be there when a hatchling turned bottom-up, which it would do only right after a feeding, to produce a white blob from its cloaca. This was the chick's excrement, or droppings. These droppings, unlike those of adult birds, came out sealed in a white sac – nature's neat disposal bag. The hen snatched up the white pellet and swallowed it. This kept the nest from becoming fouled and might also be a useful re-cycling system, since the pellet still contained some nutrients, not fully absorbed by the young chick's digestive tract. Not much went to waste in this nest.

A pellet for disposal.

Smooth cooperation: he fed a chick, she stood back . . .   *she fed two others, he stood back . . .*

During the first week the hen hardly ever left the young alone in the nest. When she wanted to have a few minutes off for an excursion outside she waited until the cock arrived with one of his food deliveries which he kept up at the rate of about once every three to four minutes. Instead of giving him her usual greeting she hopped to the back of the nest and the two parents silently looked at each other. Then she darted out. Their exchange of looks seemed like a goodbye nod. He knew she was leaving and she saw that he remained behind. Being left alone with the young brought out the cock's paternal behaviour. From the first day he leaned over them just like the hen, and pleaded with the same chirp. At first his call was less persistent than hers. He got no responses and when the hen returned he gave her his caterpillar and turned the job over to her. Yet, every time he was alone with the chicks he tried again. Here he had patiently stood over a line-up of firmly closed beaks. It looked most unpromising. Then one small body stirred on the far side and a gaping beak was offered up. The cock immediately responded and with perfect precision aimed his beak into the open mouth. To do it he had to lean precariously over the row of sleepers. He nearly lost his foothold but was able to catch himself in the instant with one wing beautifully fanned out, while the row of sleepers slept on undisturbed *(opposite)*.

It was equally beautiful to watch the smooth cooperation between the parents in the care of the young. This was the all-important pay-off from the pair bond. When the hen returned this time, it was the first time we saw her bringing back a caterpillar. As she arrived, the cock was just feeding a chick. She stood back until he had finished. Then she moved up and fed her caterpillar to another chick while the cock stood back and watched. The hen fed a portion of her caterpillar to one chick, and a second portion to another. Those two chicks dropped off to sleep, but meanwhile the one fed a few moments earlier by the cock presented its backside and produced a white pellet. The hen picked it up as the cock leaned forward and watched. Next, another chick also produced a pellet, a much bigger one, and the cock took his turn. He took the pellet under the watchful eye of the hen, and flew out with it. Then the hen settled herself over the chicks who still needed her warmth, especially after she had been away from the nest for a while.

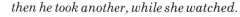

she took a pellet, as he watched . . .   *then he took another, while she watched.*

The hen with a prize catch . . .

the cock with a green 'moustache'.

More Food Please!

In their second week the young chicks grew to be much more active and bigger – and so did the caterpillars. This was proof that hen and cock had got the seasonal timing right. At this age the hen began to leave the young on their own for short periods, and she went out to collect food for them along with the cock. He had just found a fat caterpillar which curled like a green moustache around his beak. The cock's crest feathers were raised which showed that he was alarmed by something, perhaps a rival bird, which kept him from flying over to the nestbox. The hen was in a near-by tree stretching up to look all around. She had a prize catch of two caterpillars in her beak.

When the cock arrived at the nest he stopped on the perch and looked in. The young perceived the slight knock of his landing. Three heads instantly shot up and three beaks opened wide. Inside each orange mouth we could see the distinctive white markings which all such chicks have. These markings are thought to make the bright mouths even more eye-catching to the parents, and may serve as the target point at which they aim their beaks. For the very first time we could hear a faint, high-pitched *cheep . . . cheep . . . cheep* coming from the throats of the nestlings. They were beginning to be able to give voice to 'food please!' and this will move their parents to bring them more and more.

Another sign of progress was the grey stubble of feathers sprouting on their heads, along their spines, and at the edges of their wings. This first show of feathers, enclosed in hollow, hard sheaths, became visible on about the ninth day after hatching. These pin-like feathers grew out so fast that one of the first hatched chicks, in front to the right, already had considerably more stubble than the one to the left which was merely about fifty or sixty hours younger. With the advantage of these few hours, the older one's eyelids were beginning to come unsealed and we could see a slit of eye.

Three chicks giving voice to 'food please!' as the cock looked in.

In their steady collaboration the two parents sometimes returned from the food hunt together. This time the cock had entered first, and backed aside to make room for the hen. The pair stood looking down at their brood: where to start with three such equally appealing cheeping mouths facing them?

Cave-digging hen.

The parents stood so high above the young because the hen had taken up a major reconstruction of the nest. The cup had already become deeper and larger through the weight of eggs and hen, and all her wigglings and shufflings. This week she gave up tossing her chicks and switched to a new cave-digging activity. We frequently found her tunnelling with all her might, using feet, body and wings to excavate into the nest material. This changed the cup into a much wider area surrounded by steep walls which fenced in the chicks while giving them sufficient space for movement. If the hen had not done this, the fast-growing nestlings would probably have tried to move out of the smaller nest cup by now. This would have put them in danger of becoming lost in the nest material, becoming chilled, or being overlooked at feeding time. The hen's cave-digging may have been triggered by the changed activities and greater size and weight of her chicks. Perhaps she simply did it for her own comfort to make room for herself to sit next to her pin-feathered brood. They had become much too large for her to spread herself over them but they still required her brooding warmth to some extent. They needed it less than before because their bodies were beginning to produce their own warmth. This came together with the hen's downy feathers growing back on her brood patch. Hormones to make these feathers grow again were gradually taking over from those that had made them fall out. The brood patch was still sensitive to the chicks' skin temperatures, and the hen would sit with them for longer periods on chilly days to give them warmth. She also still slept with them at night.

When the hen heard the cock's greetings outside she rushed to the nest hole to lean out and seemed to take him by surprise when he landed.

Sometimes the hen hovered at the nest hole with fluttering wings to receive a cater-pillar from the cock outside. Then she turned to her begging chicks who had also been quick to perceive the cock's arrival. Their main communication with their parents was by sound and feel, and while their eyes were still closed, the ear openings were fully formed on their naked heads from the start. In the normally dim light of an enclosed nest, hearing and perception of vibration are much more useful and reliable senses than vision. It makes sense therefore that animals born and raised in such dark hidden places can generally hear before they can see, according to their inborn schedule of physical body development.

She fed a pin-feathered chick. Its ear openings were prominent, its eyes just starting to open.

After meals a chick usually turned bottom-up to produce a pellet which the parent extracted ...

The hen waited after the feeding, and a chick duly produced a pellet. The hen no longer swallowed these. She neatly extracted the pellet and carried it out, well away and out of sight of the nest where she probably dropped it. It was inborn to both parents to have to fly a certain distance before wanting to dispose of the pellet. This habit was a great help to the safety of the brood because a trail of pellet litter near the nest could have advertised it to enemies. A double purpose was served: keeping the pellets from dropping out of sight into the nest was essential for sanitation; carrying them well away helped to preserve the secrecy of the site.

... and carried out.

The cock's caterpillar was too big to go down (above) ... the hen entered with a smaller one (below).

The cock one day came in with the largest caterpillar we had yet seen. He tried to stuff it down a chick. The chick was willing, the cock tried patiently, but the caterpillar was winning. It refused to go down. Such a big caterpillar had jaws which could cling to the mouth of the chick and we later often saw the parents bashing the bigger caterpillars on a tree branch to break their jaws or kill them before bringing them to the nest. But this caterpillar was lively. The cock gave up on chick number one, and was about to try his luck with another when the hen entered and queued up behind him. He quickly took the opportunity to stand back and let her proceed while he held on to his uncooperative caterpillar. The hen hopped to the far side of the box and with immediate success fed her more dainty morsel to the chick with whom the cock had failed.

He stood aside (above)... then gave his big problem to her (below).

Before she had a chance to move away, the cock leaned across, thrust his hefty grub into her beak, and himself made a hasty exit. He left her holding the nasty caterpillar, with not even a single interested customer in sight. The hen finally solved the problem by using the cutting edge of her beak to divide the big meal into two more manageable portions, and fed these separately to two chicks whose appetites had returned. After collecting a pellet, the hen departed and crossed paths with the cock already on his way back with the next delivery. The two parents never stopped working. The seven chicks hardly ever stopped eating and they thrived and changed rapidly during the last few days of May.

Half Way

By the end of May the nest was filled with bright-eyed, flapping chicks and we could hear their little cheeps and chirps at our window all day long. Every minute or two the sound rose up in a chorus of food-begging at the arrival of a parent. It was hard to imagine that, less than two weeks ago, this lively crew had each come out of an egg as small as the two left-over ones which here have come to the surface at the front of the nest.

The chicks could now see the entering parent and the older ones no longer gaped so blindly straight up. They tried to turn their heads towards the source of food, and the one at the front left was already attempting a slight food-begging wing flutter along with its cheeping. However, the wings of the nestlings were much less finished than the already long, nearly adult legs. Their inborn schedule of body development put legs before wings. Long legs were an advantage right now for stretching up in the food queue, while wings will be needed only when the time comes to leave the nest. However, the chicks were so light-footed that two of them could sleep on soundly while the five others clambered over them.

Although there was such enthusiastic competition for food we never saw any fighting among the nestlings. Like their parents they got along peacefully. Hostility evidently was not a part of their inborn behaviour, at least not within the family. During the pauses between feedings some chicks quietly dozed while others chirped and moved about, stretched their new wings, or pecked at the wooden walls and at the nest material.

78

Unfinished wings could not yet lift the little birds.

As soon as they could see, they also wanted to peck, which would probably help their accuracy later on in the outside world when they will have to be able to pick up their own food. In the midst of these homely activities a small pair of wings would suddenly rise up in a cartwheel, breaking the air with a *brrrt* sound, as the other chicks took cover. These wing-fanning movements came together with the growth of wing feathers, yet as far as we could see only the more vigorous older chicks ever got enough air space to try, crowding out the younger ones. But even without any chance for practice, all of them will be able to fly, an ability which will come of itself when the feathers are ready. At this stage, however, there were still far too many bare patches and gaps between the flight feathers. The wings did not lift the little birds off the ground, nor even up onto the hillside of the nest. The hen was doing her job well and daily dug the cave deeper, which made the walls steeper. This gave the nestlings more room while still keeping them safely in their place.

79

TWO DAYS: *Big mouth for big meals. Blind, and naked except for tuft of headfeathers. Crawling may help in hatching. Drawing pin shows how small chick was.*

FIVE DAYS: *Weighed four times more than at hatching. Eyes still sealed by lids but ear holes fully open. Legs ahead of wings in growth. Crawling has stopped.*

The feathered chicks looked pretty to us but had seemed strange and not very attractive before. This was probably because we rarely see any animals at their earliest stages of development. Many are still inside their mothers, or still inside an egg, or hidden away in secret places like nesting holes. Therefore our birds looked so unfamiliar that they had seemed unbirdlike up to now. But of course they were blue tits from the start. It was a special period in their lives because each day they had to be fit not only to survive but above all to grow and change, hour by hour. They needed to be

FLIGHT FEATHERS: *At ten days (left) the wing feathers, here enlarged, started to break through their sheaths and looked like paint brushes. Four days later (right) the feathers had emerged but not yet sufficiently for flying.*

NINE DAYS: *Eyes open half-way. Sheathed 'pin feathers' growing fast on head, back, tail and wings – which chicks sometimes fanned (see enlargements, left below).*

TWO WEEKS: *Eyes wide open; smooth feathers; more pointed beak. Chick showing slight alarm reaction by trying to disappear, crouching down with legs tucked under.*

nearly all mouth and belly at first to grow quickly. Then their development switched to getting ready for flying and outdoor life. To get a close view of how the chicks grew we gently lifted one of them out of the nest every few days to photograph it by itself – while we were very careful to keep the parents from seeing us doing it – and then we always put the chick safely back again. Here is a blue tit's 'baby book' of photographs; all showing the chick at life size:

SIXTEEN DAYS: *Alarm caused raised crest feathers. The chick seemed torn between crouching and wanting to take flight. It was nearly ready to leave its nest.*

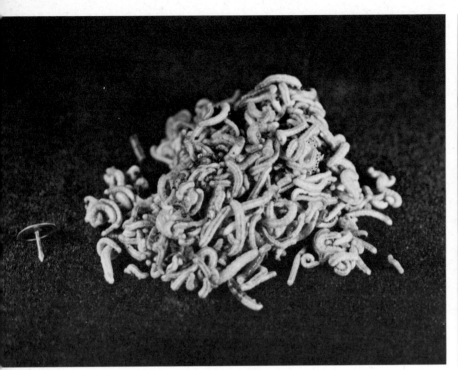

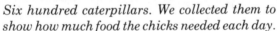

Six hundred caterpillars. We collected them to show how much food the chicks needed each day.

Caterpillar on a leaf edge (centre above) was hard to see, yet birds found them in split seconds (opposite).

Mountains of caterpillars went into turning seven naked hatchlings into seven feathered birds. To be adequately fed the nestlings together had at least 600 and often more than 1000 caterpillars each day. This added up to a grand total of 15,000 or more by the time they left the nest. With the feast of insects the hen had required in order to produce eggs, and all the insects she and the cock were eating at other times – and all the insects the many other bird families all around us needed – one could easily see what a disaster people's use of insecticides can be to bird life. It also showed us how well birds can reduce caterpillar numbers. They could never kill them all because there are usually hundreds of thousands of grubs on a good-sized tree and plenty of them escape detection. They grow into moths which lay many millions of eggs to hatch and lead to more bird life spring after spring. Each year the caterpillars eat away at the tender new leaves which are the trees' contribution to the food cycle from leaf, to insect, to bird life.

Many kinds of birds have depended on the existence of insects for so many millions of years that they have developed a whole network of links to them, such as the inborn need for the specific seasonal go-ahead signals. There are also purely physical, nutritional links. Our nestlings, like most newborn animals, could live and grow only on their own special formula of 'mother's milk'. For them, caterpillars were that formula. They needed the particular balance of proteins, minerals, vitamins and water which the caterpillars contained in an easily digestible form.

The parents too needed insects for their own nutrition and not merely as a go-ahead signal for breeding. They too needed softer foods than they would at other times of the year, because their own stomachs had changed with sexual maturing. From late summer through autumn and winter, their stomachs had been large, muscular, and loaded with grit to grind up shelled foods like seeds and nuts. Birds have no teeth; their stomachs have a gizzard, a section which contains grit and stones to function like a mill. Our birds' winter stomachs took up a large part of their abdomen while their internal reproductive organs were quite small. During February and March, when their hormones had started up sexual development, this was accompanied by a gradual shrinking of the stomach. Eventually cock and hen had a summer stomach. It was small and flabby, and fit only for digesting soft foods, while most of the space in the abdomen was given over to the greatly enlarged ovary in the hen, and the greatly enlarged testicles in the cock. Insects were therefore a most suitable food preference for the parents' tender summer stomachs, as well as being the right food for the young. As with almost everything we saw, the needs of the parents and the needs of their young were tied together. Knowing how much the parents liked insect food themselves, made us realize how overwhelming their urge to feed the young must have been. Otherwise the parents might have neglected the needs of their chicks and stayed in the trees for leisurely day-long picnics for themselves.

When the parents found a well-stocked tree, they concentrated on it, commuting back and forth to the nest, until they had to look for the next good shopping place. Among the most handsome sights to see were their mid-air pickups. Cock and hen were able to manoeuvre so precisely that they could fly right up to the edge of a leaf where they had spotted a caterpillar. They hovered for a split second, without setting their feet down, grabbed their prey, and flew straight back to the nest with it. In flight these otherwise small and dainty birds had an impressively wide and powerful wing beat, which carried them many hundreds of miles. The cock alone probably covered more than two thousand flight miles during the weeks of our acquaintance with him.

The two parents worked fifteen hours a day from dawn until well after eight at night. They had a short time to themselves in the early daylight and then made up for this with special bursts of activity in mid-morning, and again around noon, and also from late afternoon till early evening. A week after hatching, when the hen began to do her share of food-finding, we found that one or other parent turned up with food in the nest about once every minute during peak feeding hours. Even during the more leisurely periods of the day, a parent appeared every three to five minutes, except for a somewhat lazier spell in the early afternoon.

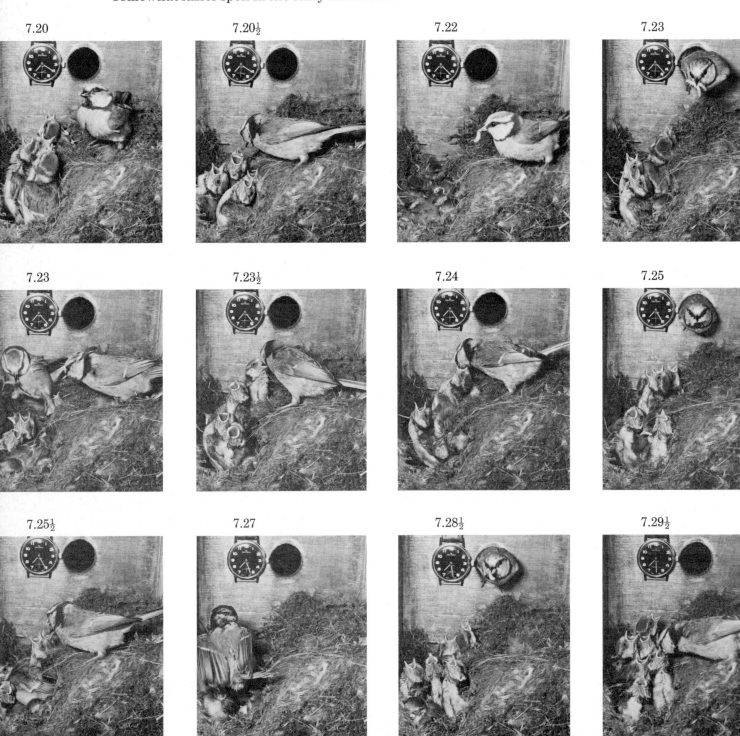

7.20   7.20½   7.22   7.23

7.23   7.23½   7.24   7.25

7.25½   7.27   7.28½   7.29½

To prove the frequency of visits, we tacked a watch to the back of the nestbox. We would not have done this earlier in the season because it certainly would have caused the hen to abandon our box. But we were confident that we could now count on her attachment to the chicks to keep her here, although it might take a while for her to become accustomed to the new object. The chicks themselves paid no attention to it. When the hen arrived and first heard the ticking, and saw the watch, she flew away without feeding any chick. She soon returned, stopped on the perch and looked in, particularly at the watch. The young were gaping and calling, but the hen hesitated just as the cock had done when he first came to visit her in the empty box. The hen flew away again. She came back, and flew away, and came back. Finally, the watch no longer worried her so much and the call of her young strongly drew her in. It took a while longer for the cock to accept the watch, but within about an hour both parents were coming and going as if nothing new had happened. We left the watch there, and two days later when we had seen that the parents' normal routine was not at all upset by it, we took the photographs on the opposite page.

It was the last day of May, early in the evening, always one of the busier times of day for the parents. It turned out to be a quite typical one. We started at 7.20 and took a photograph only when either the hen, or the cock, or both, arrived with food. In the first three minutes, three deliveries were made. Then, at 7.23 the cock flew in with two caterpillars and the hen arrived with a third, which were fed to the chicks in half a minute. This speedy catering service provided the chicks with fourteen caterpillars in the ten minutes shown here from 7.20 to 7.30 – an average of one caterpillar every forty-three seconds. The parents managed all this while also stopping regularly in between to pick up and carry out the chicks' pellets – which we did not photograph. We continued to time the comings and goings for another half hour, and the parents continued steadily at the same pace. Imagine being such a cock and hen, finding and picking up so many caterpillars so quickly, and also having to cover the daily miles of flight on the way.

The amount of interest shown by the chicks had a profound effect on the parents. Occasionally, all the chicks were satisfied and none called or gaped when a parent arrived. Then the parents would stay away for a few minutes, taking time to have a quick meal for themselves, until the young were up and calling again. But sometimes the young suddenly fell silent even when they were hungry. By now they were able to respond to distant sounds outside. When they heard the cock giving his special *drrrt . . . drrrt . . . drrrt* alarm call as he sat in a tree, with crest feathers raised, they all instantly put their heads down like soldiers in a trench, and not a cheep was heard until the alarm calls stopped.

Getting Ready

In the first seven days of June our birds grew to be so big and bold, so plump and handsomely feathered, that they outshone and at times towered over their parents. Meanwhile, the parents were becoming frayed from their miles of flight and from taking little interest in looking after themselves. The time for that will come later when there will no longer be such an eager family to welcome them.

When the hen here arrived with two caterpillars she was briefly overwhelmed by the excitement and noise, with four loud, bright mouths turned towards her. She gave the first caterpillar to the chick with the widest food-begging wing flutter whereupon the chick standing next to it redoubled its efforts to gain her attention and looked quite like an outraged bully. The hen obliged, and calmly fed her second caterpillar to that insistently begging chick.

Gone were the quiet days of gentle gaping and mild cheepings. As the young became bigger they begged ever more loudly, a way of asserting that they still needed their parents very much. The more food-begging noise the chicks made, the more food they got. This was greatly to their advantage. However, the same noise which was so necessary for attracting the parents would sound like a dinner bell to any hungry weasel or cat, or other prowler passing by. The chicks' sudden silence, whenever they heard the cock's alarm calls (*page 85*), helped to reduce this risk. Nevertheless, with each noisy day the dangers increased that the protective shelter of the nest could turn into a death trap.

The young were passing the period of greatest advantage in being dependent on their parents in the enclosed nest. Having grown this far it was now advantageous for them to get on and out. There were not only the increasing dangers from outside invaders. The protected warm quarters which were such a good place for breeding birds, were also good for breeding germs and parasites, carrying the risk of outbreak of diseases. This is why the disposal of the chicks' pellets by both parents, and the hen's daily cleanups of the nest, were such important behaviours towards reducing rotting rubbish and parasites. Therefore, in spite of the risks, the great majority of nestlings raised in an enclosed shelter get a good start in life and fly out healthy and fit. Their toughest time will come then, and only about twenty out of every hundred of these new birds will still be alive by the end of summer. The totally new life outdoors will be hard on our birds as they will have to start finding their own food and may face hunger, unaccustomed hazards, aloneness, cold nights, wind and rain. During this, their third week, they became as ready as possible for the challenge ahead.

She was briefly overwhelmed by the competing chicks (above) . . .
when she fed the first (below), the next in line looked outraged.

Services kept up: steady food deliveries on a soaking wet day . . .   *regular pellet removals . . .*   ▶

Although the nestlings had grown as big as adults, the parents never treated them as such. After each feeding the parents still kept up their pellet-disposal services. The hen still spent a lot of time diving in among the young, and kept up nest sanitation. Sometimes she gently preened her chicks, probably picking out parasites. During this week she gave up sleeping at night in the crowded nest and took up an outdoor roost near by, and near the cock. But during the day she still liked to nestle in among her chicks. Since mother and young were now about the same size, we could tell her apart mainly by her brighter colours, her longer and more pointed beak, and her slim long tail distinct from the chicks' short and stubby ones.

This week the chicks' vague cheeps and chirps developed into a more definite brisk exchange with one another of a *di . . . di . . . dit* sound, and they also began to respond

Stretching a wing and struggling up . . .   *to finally conquer the hillside . . .*   ▶

the hen preening a chick's head . . .

and nestling in with the big chicks behind her.

with this call to a matching one heard from the parents outside. They were establishing a contact call between one another which will be most useful for keeping the family together in their life outdoors. They also started up a high-pitched *zip-zip-zip* background noise. We did not know what that meant but heard an echo of it from other newly fledged bird families which were beginning to populate the trees outside.

The young were already well able to preen their own feathers with inborn skill, which will be needed soon to keep their flight machinery in good repair. The oldest chicks made determined efforts to conquer the hillside of moss and finally succeeded, but looked ever so helpless and forlorn at the top. The look of helplessness changed to promising competence two days later when one of the older chicks spread its wings wide, much wider than they had reached last week. This chick looked ready for take-off.

two days later, with wings spread wide . . .

looking ready to go.

Cock and greeting chorus.

We expected that the young would soon leave us. Nineteen days had gone by since hatching, and these birds usually fly from the nest when they are about three weeks old. The exact date depended to some extent on the weather. A rainy day would probably put them off.

The parents kept on bringing food steadily and the greeting chorus became louder than ever. This time, when the cock arrived the chicks all tried to turn their cheeping mouths towards him, but only the one nearest to him succeeded. The others were misled because they saw the cock's reflection mirrored in our blacked-out window and they were pointing towards his reflected image – just as we can sometimes see ourselves reflected in a shop window when the space behind the window is dark. Thus three open mouths were pointed towards us. The message of the gaping mouths was easy to understand and gave even us a strong feeling of wanting to feed the chicks. By now the bright flange around their beaks was disappearing and they had proper hard beaks which will help them to catch their own food outdoors. Their new diet there will be mainly greenflies and other small insects which were becoming increasingly plentiful, while the caterpillar season was already coming to its end.

That evening we left the young snuggled together. It was a rare event to be able to count all seven heads, all except one wide awake. The oldest and boldest chick clearly had the nest hole and the world beyond in view. This turned out to be their last night under one roof.

Their last night together.

Taking Off

'Here I am, I'm coming! No . . . I'm not.' The oldest and boldest of the chicks was leaning out of the nest hole early the following morning, the seventh day of June. The chick called *di. . .di. . . .dit* loudly and the contact replies came back from the cock high up in a near-by tall tree. The chick daringly leaned further out and seemed ready to go. But no, it suddenly took fright, its crest feathers went up in alarm and it stopped calling.

It was a hectic day for the parents who organized the move. The weather was fine, they got an early start, and got the whole family under way by noon, including the youngest stragglers. The cock established a tree-top reception station, about forty feet up in the dense canopy of leaves. He stayed there and kept up a steady voice contact with the nest. The hen alone whizzed back and forth to continue to bring food to the nest every few minutes. She herself looked frazzled and thin but the chicks came first. Their immediate need was still greater than hers.

As soon as the leading adventurer was fed again, the lure of the outside world drew it back to the nest hole. It kept on fluttering up to get a foothold and look out, and the next in line became stirred up too and joined in with the contact calling. The first chick looked ready to step out onto the perch but quickly withdrew back inside. Such wavering, between uncertainty and the temptation to go, went on for more than half an hour with a steadily increasing exchange of contact calls between cock and chick. Finally, as the intensity of the calls mounted to almost a frenzy, the chick seemed carried away by the excitement, and in one quick move launched itself into the air. Its wings went into action and carried the chick steeply upwards and out of our sight. It kept on giving its contact call all the way up. When that changed to the sound of a food-begging greeting, high up among the leaves, we knew it had arrived safely by the side of the cock.

Thin and frazzled hen continuously brought food . . .

one chick fluttered up; the next showed interest.

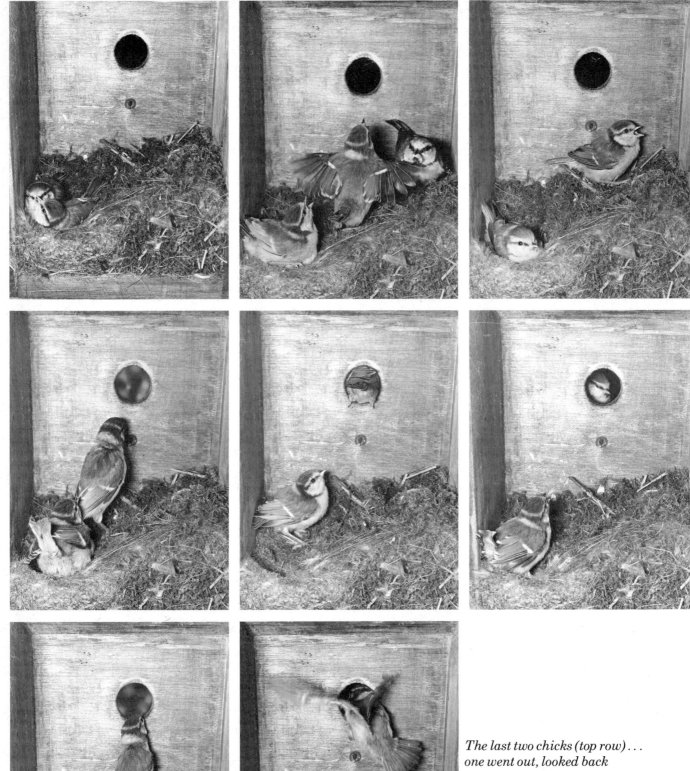

The last two chicks (top row) . . . one went out, looked back briefly (above) . . . and the other followed in a hurry.

'Wait for me!'

The next four fledglings followed more or less in order of age, until only the two youngest and smallest were left. They cowered together. The hen came with food and one of the chicks rushed to greet her. This was perhaps its first opportunity to spread its wings freely because earlier it had been crowded out by the older ones. When the hen had gone, the nearly deserted nest offered little comfort. The little chick did not go to sleep as had been customary after a meal. It hopped about restlessly, and called and called. From outside, the cock responded and the recent nest leavers, who were with him, added their own contact calls. The stubby-tailed chick hopped up to the nest hole and with none of the uncertainty its elders had shown, it went right out onto the perch, merely turned its head back for one brief last look in, and then flew up high as well as all the others but not yet with quite the elegant smooth wing sweep of the parents in flight.

One alone was left. It made up its mind in a hurry. The empty nest may have seemed a stranger place than the space outside where the familiar voices called. The last one went up to the nest hole, and without any hesitation at all it flew out and up, calling all the way 'here I come . . . here I come . . . wait for me!'

95

The chick (left) landed facing the hen.

The Future

The last and smallest of the chicks landed about forty feet up, near the top of the same rugged, old tree where we had seen the parents on their way to mating, towards the end of April. Here, on June 7th, was the result. By inborn ability this chick had been able to fly, able to land, able to perch on a branch – all actions it had never done before. The chick also 'knew' where it wanted to go. But not quite accurately: it had slightly missed its goal and still found itself alone. The cock had progressed with the first group of young to a tree farther on. The hen was nearer, sitting equally high up in another tree, about ten feet away, with two other fledglings. The lone chick called. The hen called back, but stayed where she was and kept on calling to the chick. The chick fluffed its wings, leaned forward, leaned back again, fluffed its wings again, and finally took the plunge to cross the great gulf of air. It landed safely beside the hen and was welcomed with a mouthful of food from her.

That night there was heavy rain. It was a relief on the following morning to hear the voices of our pair and the cheeping of the young, sounding as lively as ever after their first night out. But they stayed so high up, concealed among the leaves, that we could not keep count of the chicks. We were never sure how many survived over the next days although we continued to listen and look out for them. We saw that the cock and hen were always with a group of young and still fed them to some extent, while each day the fledglings became better at finding their own food. The whole group wandered from tree to tree, sometimes with one parent leading an advance party ahead, while the second parent stayed behind with the others. They kept up constant contact calling to each other, their way of conveying 'I'm here, come along' or 'I'm here, wait for me'. This helped them to stay together.

After two weeks the family left our neighbourhood. The fledglings were ready to take the next step; they felt the urge to fly away, each on its own, to join one of the many roaming flocks of birds, young and old mixed together. The parents, too, flew off and returned to their own earlier way of life in a flock community. In autumn the new birds will begin to show an interest in the opposite sex and, if successful in finding mates, they will be looking for nesting sites of their own towards the end of winter. If the parents do not come back to make a first claim on their former nest, one of the young may well return to its birthplace in our window nestbox – which we hope will house new generations of blue tits each spring.